eyewonder

Weather

DK

DK Penguin Random House

Senior Art Editor Ragini Rawat
Project Editor Upamanyu Das
Editors Shahid Qureshi, Zarak Rais
Picture Researcher Ridhima Sikka
Managing Editor Kingshuk Ghoshal
Managing Art Editors Anna Hall, Govind Mittal
Pre-production Team Pawan Kumar, Mohammad Rizwan
Production Editor Anita Yadav
Senior Production Controller Ben Radley
Senior Jackets Art Editor Nehal Verma
Project Jackets Art Editor Vidushi Chaudhry
India Creative Head Malavika Talukder
Associate Publisher Gemma Farr
Art Director Mabel Chan

Consultant Adam Scaife

This edition published in 2026
First published in Great Britain in 2004 by
Dorling Kindersley Limited
20 Vauxhall Bridge Road,
London, SW1V 2SA

The authorised representative in the EEA is
Dorling Kindersley Verlag GmbH. Arnulfstr. 124,
80636 Munich, Germany

10 9 8 7 6 5 4 3 2 1
001–354830–Feb/2026

A CIP catalogue record for this book is available from the British Library.
ISBN: 978-0-2417-7735-0

Printed and bound in China

www.dk.com

MIX
Paper | Supporting responsible forestry
FSC www.fsc.org FSC™ C018179

This book was made with Forest Stewardship Council™ certified paper – one small step in DK's commitment to a sustainable future.
Learn more at www.dk.com/uk/information/sustainability

Contents

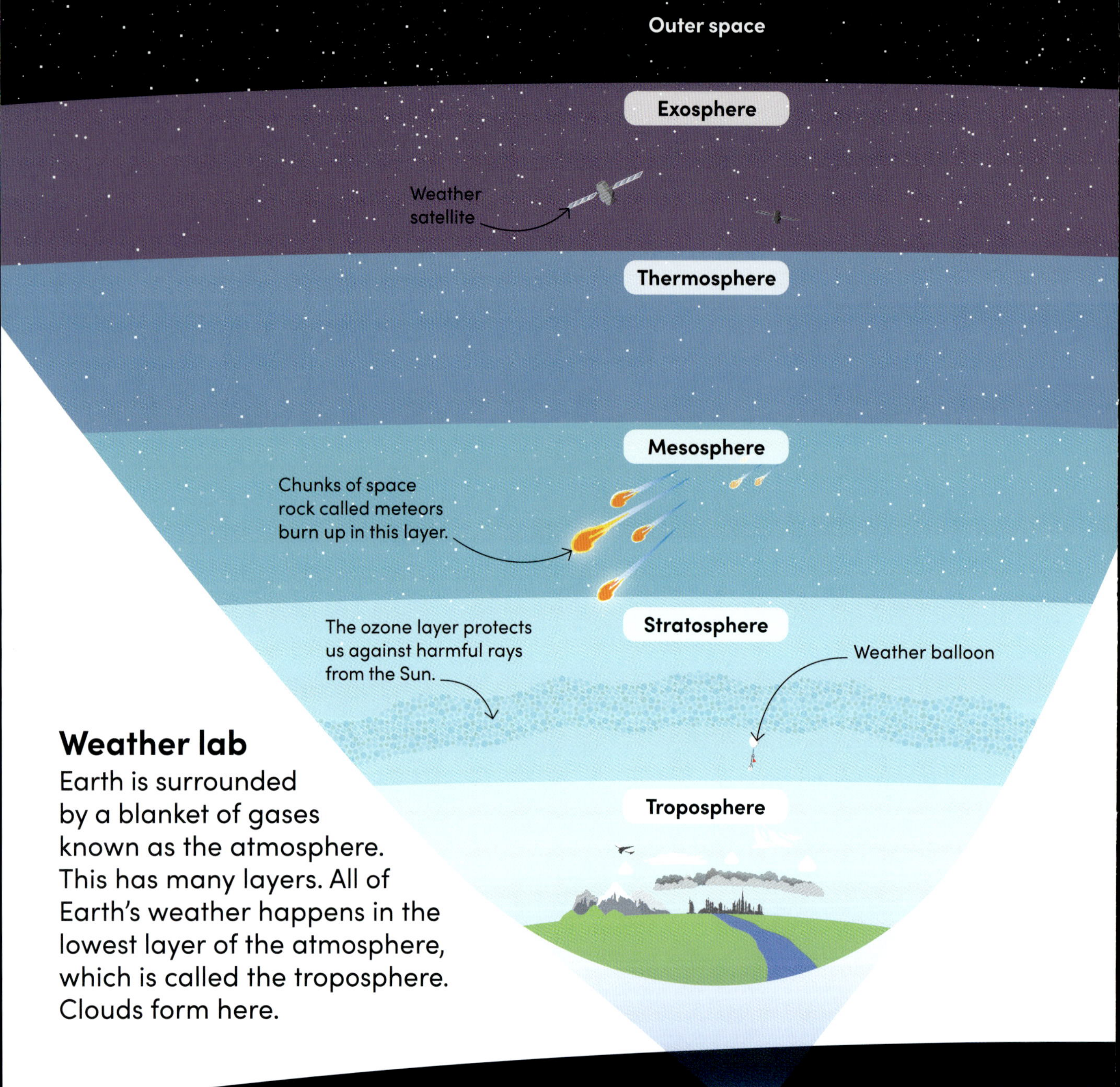

Weather lab

Earth is surrounded by a blanket of gases known as the atmosphere. This has many layers. All of Earth's weather happens in the lowest layer of the atmosphere, which is called the troposphere. Clouds form here.

What's weather?

"Weather" is what the sky and the air outside are like – cloudy, snowy, sunny, or windy. Weather happens when air gets warmer or cooler. It changes from place to place.

Fast facts

The study of weather is called meteorology. Scientists who study the weather are known as meteorologists.

Weather can change quickly – within hours or even minutes.

The outermost layer of Earth's atmosphere, the exosphere, has artificial satellites that monitor weather on the planet.

Rain or shine

The weather on any day depends on how much sunshine, wind, rain, or snow there is. A day with lots of sunshine and no wind, rain, or snow will be warm.

Sunshine

Wind

Rain

Snow

Clouds in our atmosphere look white because they reflect sunlight.

Thin skin

If Earth was an apple, the atmosphere would be its skin. It stretches just 100 km (70 miles) above the planet's surface before it gets very thin.

Changing seasons

The northern and southern halves, or "hemispheres", of the planet receive different amounts of sunlight. This is because Earth is tilted on its axis, an imaginary line drawn through the centre of our world. The two hemispheres experience different seasons at the same time.

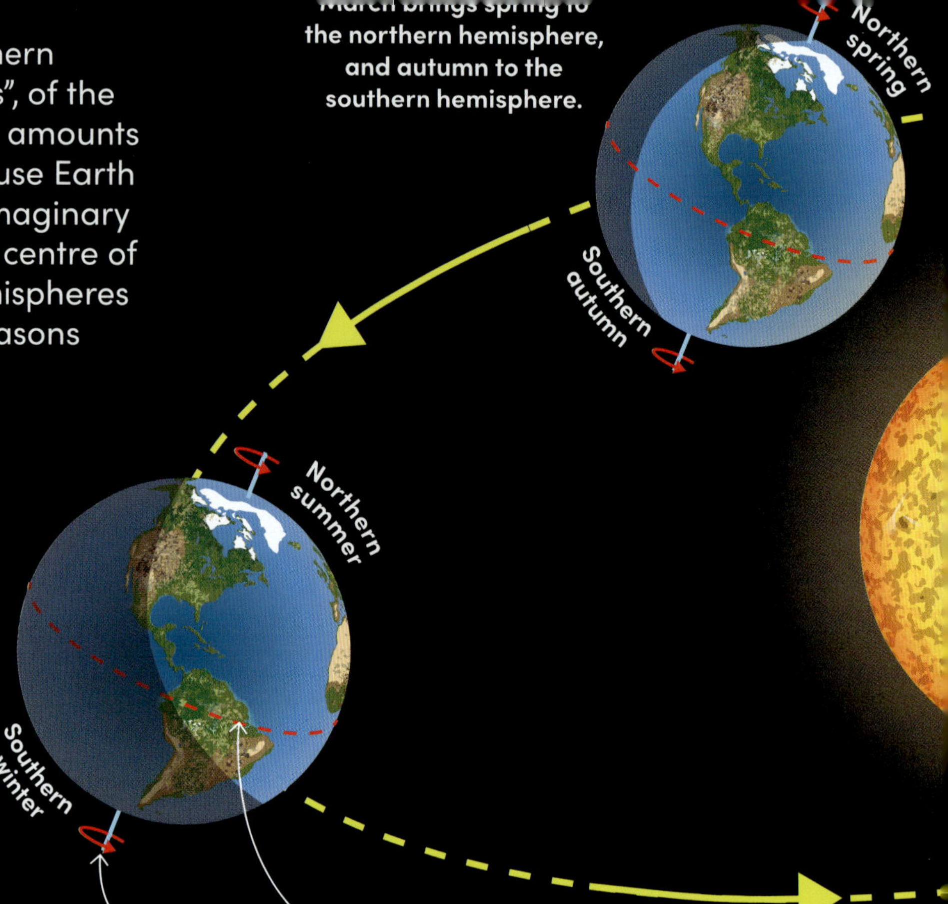

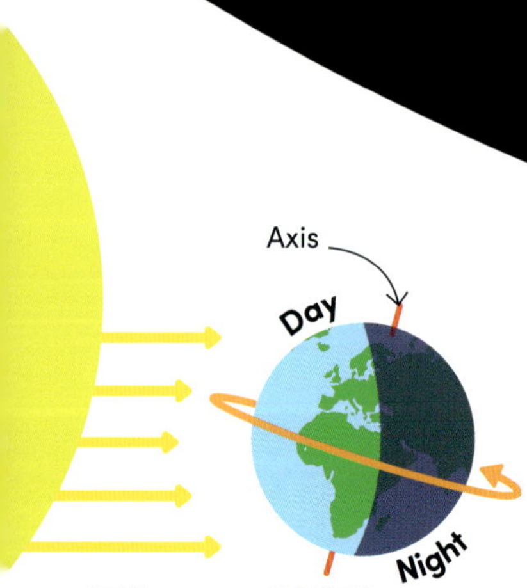

Day and night

Our planet spins (rotates) on its axis. It completes one rotation every 24 hours. It's daytime on the side facing the Sun, and night-time on the other side.

The seasons

Our planet travels around the Sun, making one loop every year. As different parts of it move in and out of the Sun's heat, they experience weather changes that last for many months – these are called seasons.

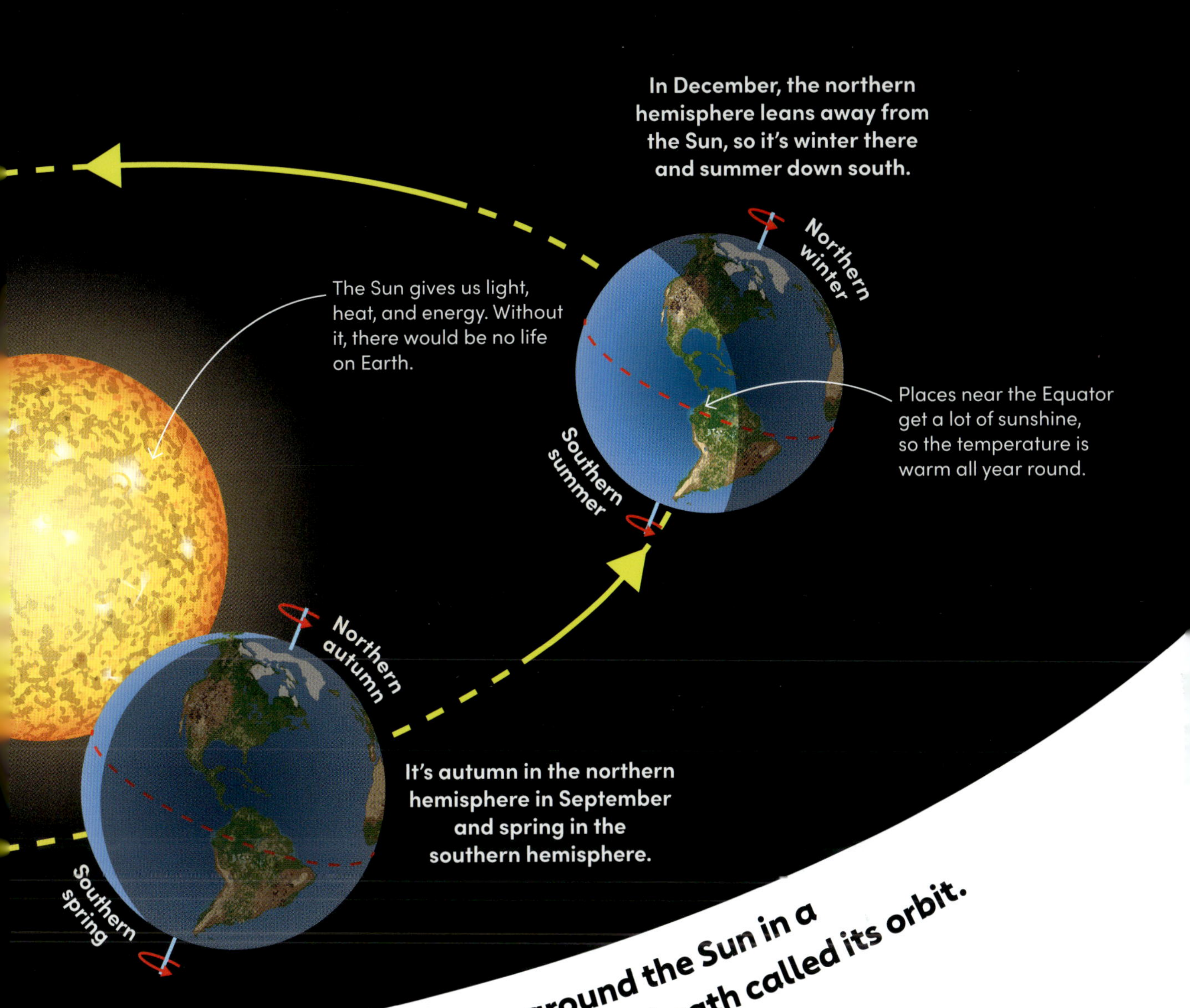

Earth loops around the Sun in a fixed path called its orbit.

PLANTS AND SEASONS

The changing seasons affect how plants grow. Most farm plants, or crops, are planted in spring and harvested in summer or autumn. But harvest time can vary from place to place, as seen here.

Spinach (spring), USA, northern hemisphere

Strawberry (summer), Australia, southern hemisphere

Onion (autumn), UK, northern hemisphere

Maize (winter), Brazil, southern hemisphere

What's climate?

Weather changes from day to day. Climate is different. It's like long-term weather – the weather patterns and temperatures an area has over a longer period of time. Different parts of the world have different climates.

Fast facts

Most places around the world have four seasons. Each season brings unique climate conditions.

The average temperature on Earth's surface is 15°C (59°F).

Earth's climate has changed over time. The "ice ages" of the past covered much more of the planet in snow.

Reading temperature

The temperature of a place tells us how hot or cold it is. Higher temperatures mean a place is hotter, and lower temperatures could mean a place is freezing cold.

Shaping climate

Earth's physical features such as high mountains or vast oceans can affect climate. A mountain range may mean the climate in the area will be cool.

Hot and wet

The areas around Earth's centre are called the tropics. Here the climate is hot and wet all year round.

Tropical cloud forest in Ecuador

Mild temperatures

Temperate climates have warm summers and cool winters. It rarely gets too hot or cold, but the weather can be stormy and unreliable.

Temperate forest in Alaska, USA

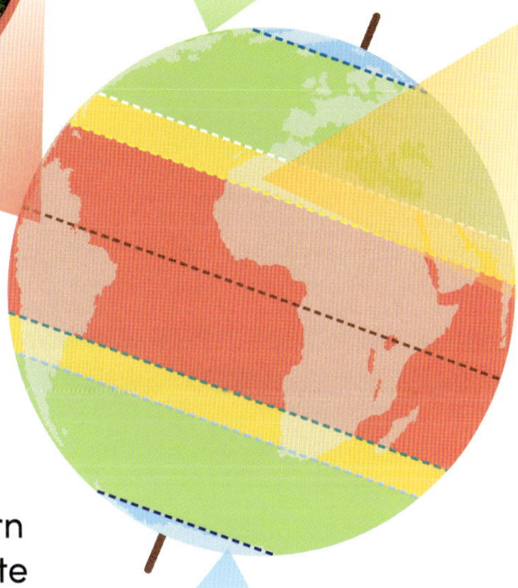

Climate zones

Earth's climate is warmest around its middle. Its coldest zones are at the poles – Earth's most northern and southern points. Climate determines what plants and animals live in a place.

- Tropical
- Subtropical
- Temperate
- Polar

Sunny and dry

Subtropical climates have hot summers and cold winters. Many of Earth's deserts, such as the Sahara, are found here.

Icy cold

It is freezing cold at Earth's North and South poles for most of the year. The ground is frozen solid around the South pole, while ice sheets float on the ocean in the north.

Coast of Antarctica, the frozen southern continent

The power of the Sun

The Sun produces huge amounts of energy. A lot of it is released into space as heat and light, which is vital for life on Earth. It also powers our planet's weather, warming up water that rises into the air before falling back down again as rain and snow.

Cooling down

As the vapour rises, it cools. Water vapour in the air turns back into water droplets and forms clouds. This process is called condensation.

Warming up

Heat from the Sun warms the water in lakes, rivers, seas, and oceans, turning it into invisible water vapour that rises into the air. This process is called evaporation. The Sun's heat also causes moisture from plants to evaporate.

Moving air

The Sun's rays warm pockets of air, making them rise upwards. Cool air then rushes in to fill the gap. This movement of air is wind.

Fast facts

Nearly all the water on Earth's surface is salty. Less than one per cent is fresh water, which may be drinkable.

Precipitation is the process in which water falls to the ground as rain or snow.

Moisture is a small amount of water in the air or on a surface.

Making rain

When the water droplets in clouds get big enough, they fall to the ground as rain. If the air is cold enough, the water freezes into snowflakes or hailstones.

Starting again

Some of the rainwater flows into rivers and then back into seas and oceans. Some of it evaporates to form clouds again. In this way, water goes around and around in a cycle.

Cirrus

High, wispy, feathery clouds are called cirrus. At great heights, the air is so cold that these clouds are made from ice crystals rather than water drops. Sometimes, strong winds blow them into long strands.

Cumulus

Plump and fluffy cumulus clouds are found at different heights. Small, white cumulus clouds often appear on sunny days, but the big, dark cumulonimbus clouds mean rain or snowstorms are on the way.

Stratus

Clouds that look like flat, grey sheets are stratus clouds. Of all the main cloud types, they are lowest in the sky. Sometimes they sit right on the ground to form fog.

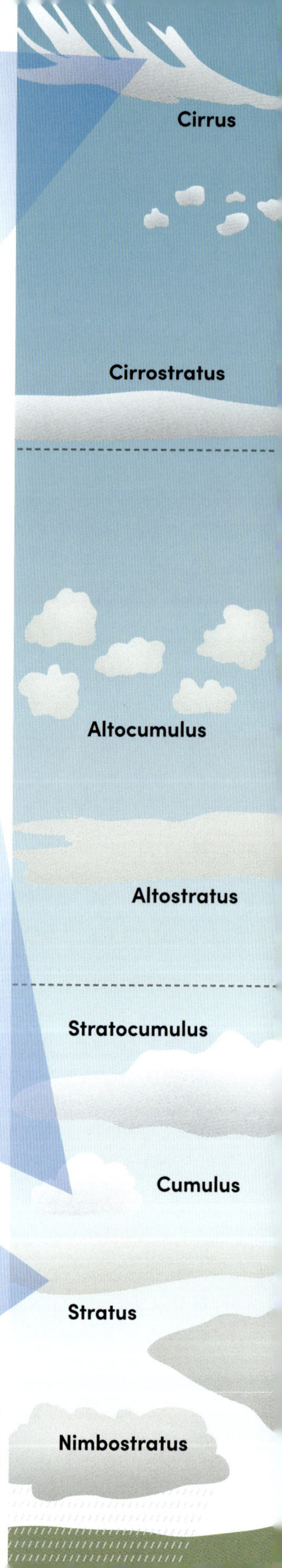

Some common cloud types

Cloudy skies

They might look a bit like cotton wool, but clouds are not solid at all. Each cloud is a collection of tiny drops of water. The three most common cloud types are stratus, cumulus, and cirrus. Clouds can combine to form other types of cloud.

Clouds with "nimbo" or "nimbus" in their name are rain clouds.

Naming clouds

Clouds are grouped according to their height, appearance, and how they're formed. For example, "Alto" clouds form at medium height. They often look like patchy sheets of white or grey with rounded shapes.

Glittering skies

Noctilucent clouds are the highest clouds in the sky, forming 80 km (50 miles) above Earth's surface. They look like soft, glowing waves that appear only rarely on summer nights, often just as the Sun sets.

Flying clouds

Lenticular clouds got their name because they look a little like lenses stacked on top of each other, but some of them look more like flying saucers!

The Golden Gate Bridge is painted orange to make it stand out against the fog.

Golden Gate Bridge, San Francisco, USA, enveloped in sea fog

Hazy seas

When warm, damp air blows across a cold ocean, the air cools and the moisture it carries condenses to become sea fog. This fog usually forms in spring.

Poison air

When fog mixes with smoke, it creates heavy, smelly air called smog, which is harmful for us to breathe. Many cities have smog – from Milan (left) in Italy to New Delhi, India.

All in a fog

Sometimes it's so foggy outside, you feel as if you're walking through a cloud. In fact, you are! Fog forms when water vapour condenses into droplets near the ground and then hangs in the air.

Fast facts

Fog can appear quite quickly when wind blows warm air across a cold surface.

Experts describe fog in terms of "visibility" – how far you can see through it.

In ordinary fog, you can see for about 1,000 m (3,000 ft).

In dense fog, you can see for less than 50 m (160 ft).

Wrapped in fog

If you happen to be on marshy land, or near a lake or river, you might be surrounded by a blanket of fog rolling in across the land. This fog is common in autumn and winter.

The thick fog can make it nearly impossible to see anything around you.

Mist forms when temperature changes quickly in the early mornings or at sunset.

Cool mist

Light mist swirls over the Eildon Hills (right) in Scotland. Mist is a fine, light type of fog. It often forms early in the morning, over land or water, then disappears as the day warms up.

Rain, rain

If you see dark clouds rumbling in the sky, rain is on its way! Rain clouds are full of water droplets. When these droplets get too heavy and can no longer hold this water, they fall to the ground as rain. The heaviest rain comes from the biggest, blackest clouds.

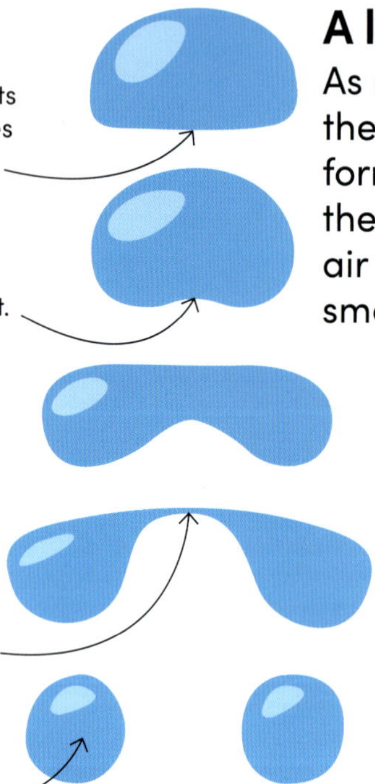

A long way down

As millions of raindrops fall down, they bump into each other and form bigger, heavier drops. But as they fall down at great speed, the air splits the large drops into smaller ones again.

Measuring rain

Scientists measure rainfall using a simple gauge set into the ground. The drops fall through the funnel at the top and are collected in the main cylinder below.

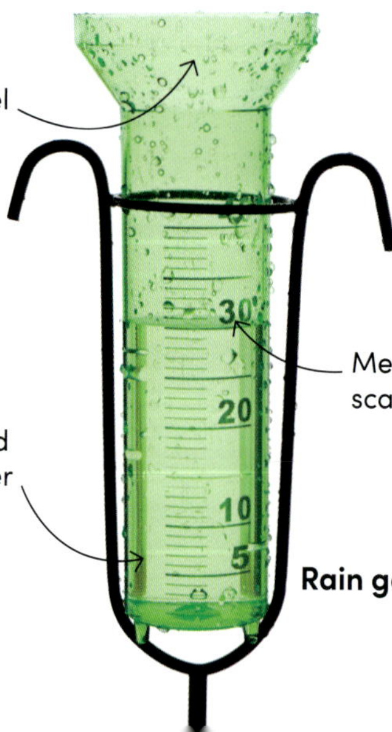

Rain gauge

VANISHING RAIN

If rain falls through extremely dry air, it can evaporate (turn from liquid into vapour) before it reaches the ground. This unusual form of rain is called virga, and it is a common sight in some deserts.

Rainy summer

Many countries get heavy rains every summer. These seasonal rains are called monsoons. Monsoon rain can fill up lakes and rivers, but too much rain can cause floods.

Bridge destroyed by an overflowing river in India

Deadly showers

Heavy downpours make rivers overflow on land. The raging waters can sweep away roads, bridges, and homes in their path.

Decorative stone

Stone damaged by acid rain

Toxic rain

Smoke from factories and cars can react with water vapour to form harmful chemicals called acids. This falls to the ground as "acid rain", which kills forests, poisons water, and even wears away stone.

White skies

When the air is cold enough, the water droplets in clouds freeze into ice. As these bits of ice grow, they bump into each other and stick together, forming snowflakes. Eventually, they fall to the ground as snow.

Look out below!
On cold mountain ranges, huge piles of snow can build up. Even a small movement can send them tumbling downhill as an avalanche.

Blizzard winds are so fast, they can make snow fall nearly horizontally.

White fury
When snow falls thick and fast in strong winds, we say there is a blizzard. The wind whips the snow up into the air, making it hard to see where you're going.

ICY ARTWORKS

Each snowflake begins as a simple six-sided shape called a hexagon, which grows six arms. What happens next may vary – it might branch out, or keep a more solid shape. There are several common designs, but the exact pattern of each snowflake is unique.

Plate shape

Column shape

Branching shape

A walkway in Tateyama Kurobe, Japan – it has some of the world's heaviest snowfalls.

Cold and dry

Some of the world's coldest places are also dry – so dry that not much snow can form. For there to be heavy snowfall, cold air must carry lots of moisture.

The snow blocks are fitted closely together, and packed with more snow.

Cosy homes

Some Inuit people from northern polar regions build small huts from blocks of snow. These temporary shelters, which they use like tents, are called igloos.

Icy showers

When solid pellets of ice fall out of the sky, we call it hail. Most hailstones are no bigger than peas, but some can be as big as apples!

Building a hailstone

Hailstones form when ice crystals get tossed up and down inside clouds. Each up-down movement adds another layer of ice to the crystal, making the hailstone grow bigger and bigger.

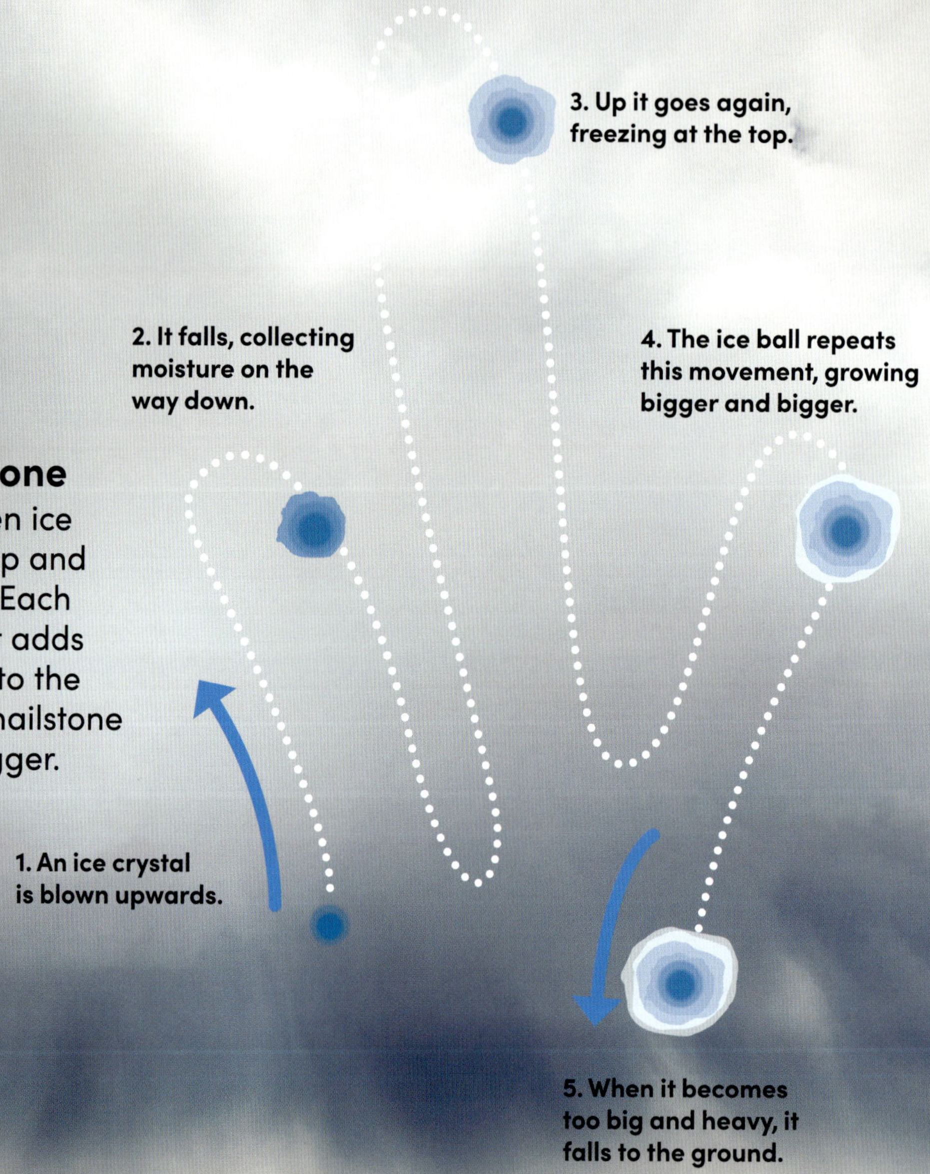

Icy missiles

Small hailstones are round and white, but bigger ones usually have knobbly shapes and jagged edges.

Big hailstones may have odd shapes made from smaller ones freezing together.

DANGER, ICE!

The most severe hail can flatten crops, smash through roofs, and even hurt animals or people. If you get caught in an extreme hailstorm, try to find some shelter indoors.

Giant hailstones can shatter the windscreen of a car caught in a hailstorm.

Road risk

Driving through a hailstorm can be dangerous. It's hard to see, the road is slippery, and really big hailstones can cause severe damage to vehicles.

Dew and frost

On cool nights, water vapour near the ground turns into water droplets, covering everything with dew drops by morning. But on really cold days, the vapour freezes into frost.

Dawn sparkle

On cool mornings, you will find glittery drops of dew covering every surface. On this delicate spider's web, the dew drops look like tiny jewels.

Smooth ice

If the temperature falls after the dew has settled, it often freezes into a covering of clear ice, like on the petals of this clover flower.

FROZEN CANDY

Hair ice is a rare type of ice that forms on damp, rotting wood. Freezing temperatures force the water out of the wood with help from a special fungus. This creates delicate, hair-like strands of ice that look like cotton candy!

Fern frost

When damp air stays in contact with cold glass, the water vapour turns directly into ice crystals. They have feathery, fern-like patterns, which give this frost its name.

Hoar frost on rose flowers

Hoar frost

As water vapour in the air touches frozen surfaces, it sometimes forms spiky ice needles instead of a smooth coating. These spikes are called hoar frost.

Rime frost can form in minutes or even seconds.

Heavy rime frost on a hawthorn tree

Rime frost builds up on the side not exposed to wind.

Rime frost

When fierce, icy winds blow cold water droplets onto solid surfaces, they freeze quickly to form rime frost. It is thick and hard, and looks like a coating of sugar.

Steady winds

A group of winds called the trade winds blow around the Equator. They blow from east to west around the tropical belt. In earlier times, people would sail from one continent to another with the help of these winds.

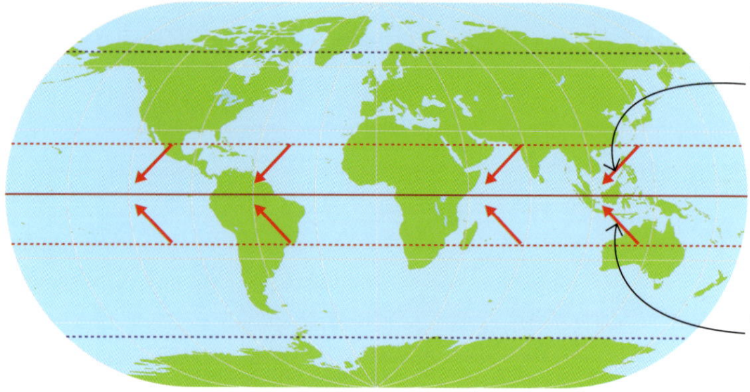

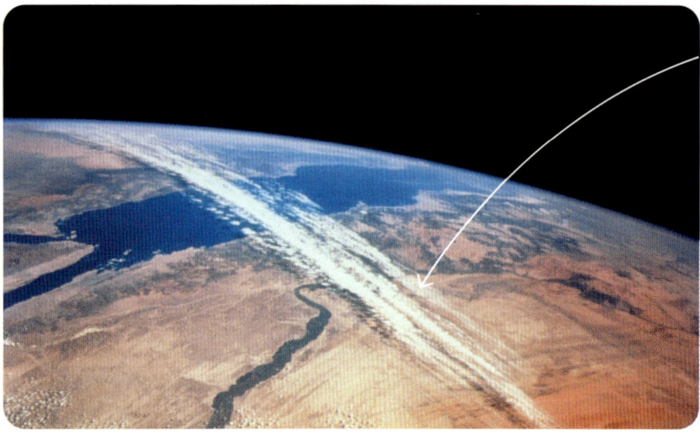

These are wispy clouds caught in the jet stream over the Sahara Desert in Egypt.

Superfast winds

Bands of high-speed winds called jet streams blow from west to east in the upper parts of the troposphere. They are so strong that pilots can cut hours off their flight times if they fly along with them.

Blowing in the wind

Air is restless and moves all the time. When it moves quickly enough for you to feel it on your face, it is called wind. Some winds blow over small areas. Other winds never stop flowing around the whole planet.

Wind-blown sand wears away the rock near the ground.

Fast facts

Wind speed is measured on the Beaufort scale. This scale has 13 points – the lowest is "calm" and the highest is a "hurricane".

When a cold wind is blowing, the temperature feels much lower than it really is. This cooling effect is called wind-chill.

Blown away

When desert sand is blown around by fierce winds, it can wear away solid rock. This leaves behind strange shapes, such as this limestone rock formation in Egypt.

The strongest winds can uproot trees easily.

Blasted sideways

It takes strong, steady winds to make a tree grow like this. The wind pushes against it day after day, so the tree grows thicker and stronger on the side facing the wind. This makes it bend away from the wind.

Electric skies

Hidden away inside clouds, very tiny bits of ice rub against each other to build up an electric charge. Then just like the crackle you may get when combing dry hair, the charge flows as a bright streak of light. This is a lightning strike.

Volcanic lightning

Lightning can also form in plumes of smoke given off in a volcanic eruption. Here, the electric charge is created by bits of ash rubbing against each other.

Volcanic lightning during an eruption of the Sakurajima volcano in Japan

Chosen paths

Lightning flashes can happen inside a cloud, between two clouds, or between a cloud and the ground. Extremely long lightning flashes are known as megaflashes.

Lightning heats up the air, making the rumble of thunder.

Danger!
Lightning is attracted to the highest nearby point on the ground below, such as a tall building or a tree. Never shelter from a storm underneath a tree!

RARE SPARKS

Red sprites are rare flashes of lightning that shoot high up into the atmosphere during some very powerful thunderstorms. They last for just a moment, and are hard to see from the ground.

Lightning storm over Newcastle, South Africa

Fiery whirl

A firenado is a hot whirl of flames whipped up by a wildfire. Firenadoes form when very hot air rises up from a fire then begins to twist, creating a spinning column of flames.

Firenado from a wildfire in Colorado, USA

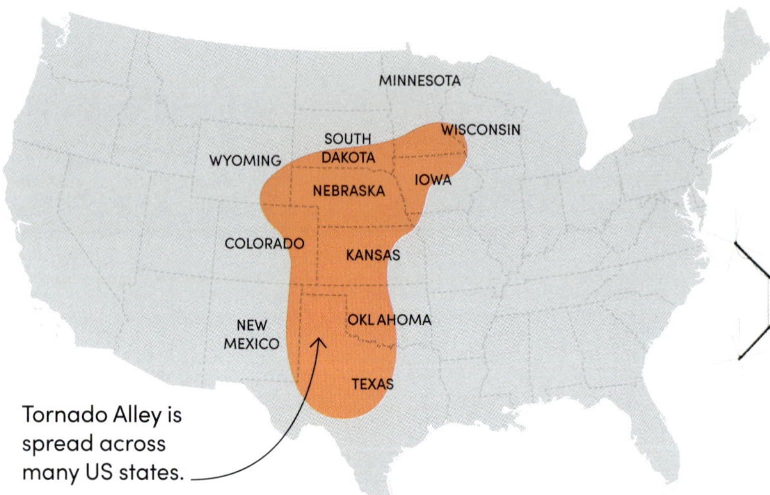

Tornado Alley

Welcome to Tornado Alley! There are more tornadoes in this region in the central part of the USA than anywhere else on Earth. Many homes in this area have underground shelters for waiting out a tornado.

Tornado in Kansas, USA

Weather monitoring truck

Tracking the twisters

Tornadoes are hard to study, but scientists track them using instruments mounted on trucks, for a quick getaway. People who follow tornadoes as they travel across the land are known as storm chasers.

Terrible twisters

Tornadoes are terrifying funnels of spinning air. They contain superfast winds with the deadly power to smash houses, flip cars over, and knock trains off their tracks.

Looming danger

Tornadoes begin as warm air drawn into the base of huge storm clouds. Warm air is lighter than cool air, so it rises quickly. As it spins faster and faster, a funnel of cloud reaches to the ground, creating a tornado.

In a tornado, winds may blow faster than 480 kph (300 mph)!

Born at sea

Tropical cyclones get their energy from warm tropical waters. They start as small storms, building into powerful swirling clouds of wind and rain. Seen here is Typhoon Kong-rey swirling over the West Philippine Sea in a satellite photo from 2024.

At the centre of the storm is its "eye". The strongest winds blow around this calm, central spot.

Deadly storms

The most devastating storms on Earth build up over warm tropical oceans. These are called tropical cyclones. They have different names: "hurricanes" over the Atlantic, "typhoons" over the Western Pacific, and "cyclones" over the Indian Ocean.

Colossal damage

Tropical storms can cause lots of damage. Typhoon Kong-rey flattened buildings and trees, flooded homes, and caused widespread power cuts.

Fast facts

Hurricanes are graded from 1 to 5. Number 1 is a storm that can cause slight damage, while 5 means a powerful storm likely to cause a potential disaster.

Typhoons often hit the Philippines, Japan, Vietnam, and southern China between early summer and late autumn.

Repair and recovery

Governments and people come together to rebuild after the damage of a tropical storm. Buildings are repaired, debris and mud cleared away, and everything made safe to use again.

Staying safe

When scientists expect a huge storm is coming, they advise people in nearby places to leave their homes. These people head to evacuation shelters for safety.

Nowhere to go

Very heavy rainfall caused England's Tewkesbury Abbey and its nearby areas to be "waterlogged" in 2024. We say an area is waterlogged when the water in it cannot flow away or drain down into the soil.

Monsoon floods

In some parts of the world, such as in Gujarat, India, the wet, rainy monsoon season often brings floods. They can appear so quickly that people don't have time to get out of the way.

Flash floods

Sometimes when warm air rises quickly to form cumulonimbus clouds over low-lying places, the thunderstorm can lead to sudden heavy rainfall. This can result in flash floods, like this one (left) in Oman.

Water, water, everywhere

Occasionally, water rises up and out of rivers and streams due to heavy rain or melting snow, and flows across the land – this is known as flooding. Floodwaters can easily submerge roads or get inside buildings.

Fast facts

Just 15 cm (6 in) of fast-moving water can knock a person off their feet.

Areas of flat land near rivers that are often flooded are known as floodplains.

Climate change is making flooding more common.

Careful at the coast!

Areas along coasts can be flooded with seawater due to storms out at sea. The water rushes inland – as seen when Hurricane Helene hit Florida, USA, in 2024.

Hurricane Helene produced winds that reached speeds of 225 kph (140 mph).

Tricks of light

Every day, the Sun puts on the best light shows on our planet. As well as multicoloured rainbows, it can create shimmering auroras, magical "sundogs", and glowing spots in the sky.

SPLITTING LIGHT

What we see as white light is made up of seven different colours. When white light is shone through a triangular block of glass called a prism, the light splits out into its seven colours.

Seeing rainbows

If the Sun is shining when rain is falling, you may see a rainbow! The drops of rain act like a prism and split the sunlight into the seven colours we see as a colourful arc in the sky. The colours are red, orange, yellow, green, blue, indigo, and violet.

A rainbow's colours always appear in the same order.

Dazzling displays

Auroras are vast sheets of bright green lights streaked with pink and blue. They appear over Earth's northern and southern polar regions. They are made by energy from the Sun.

Sundogs form when the Sun shines through ice crystals in the air.

Moondogs form when the Moon shines through ice crystals in the air.

Shining through ice

Sundogs and moondogs are bright spots of light in the sky, which form when light travels through ice crystals. The crystals act like prisms, sending the light in different directions.

Throwing shadows

A Brocken spectre occurs when someone is standing on a high point on a misty day. Their shadow is thrown into the mist, making it look like there is a gigantic person floating in the distance.

You can only see the tip of an iceberg - most of it is under water.

Floating ice

Ice floats on water because it is lighter. Icebergs are huge chunks of ice that have broken off glaciers. They can float on the ocean waters for hundreds of years.

Waterspouts

When they form at sea, whirlwinds and tornadoes are called waterspouts. Big ones can be dangerous to ships.

Tossed and turned

Thousands of ships journey across the seas and oceans. During storms, they steer straight into the waves, to stop themselves from being pushed over.

All at sea

Is there weather at sea? Definitely. Just like on land, temperature, rain, and wind all happen above the ocean. But the effects they create over water can be very different – watch out for the storms and waves!

TSUNAMI

A tsunami is a colossal wave, but it isn't a form of weather. It occurs when an earthquake shakes the ocean floor and lifts up the water to create a giant wave. Tsunamis can cause serious damage when they crash onto land.

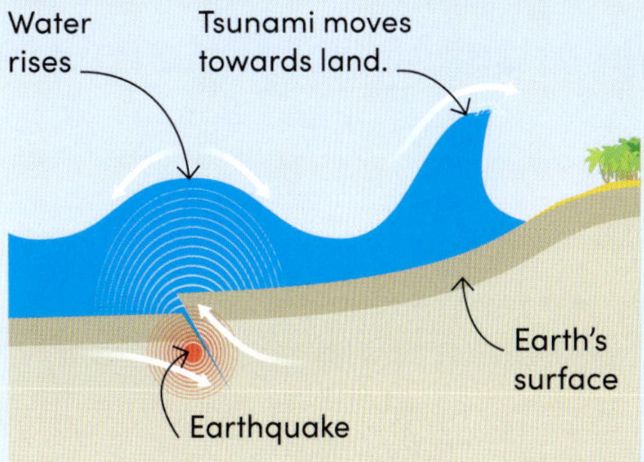

Waves crashing on the Felgueiras lighthouse in Portugal can be as tall as 10 m (33 ft)!

Winds and waves

The winds that blow over our seas and oceans can be really strong because there are no large obstacles to slow them down. These powerful winds push the water into huge waves.

Dry deserts

Rainy days are rare in the desert. Many deserts are hot and sandy, but they can be cold too. The southern continent of Antarctica is covered in ice, but it is a desert because there is little rain or snow.

Sandy stretches

Many deserts are vast areas of dry land covered with sand instead of soil. The wind blows the sand grains into shifting mounds called sand dunes.

Sand in the air

When the wind blows hard in sandy deserts, it creates swirling clouds of thick sand and dust. Sand storms are common in places that are built in or near deserts, such as Sudan.

Orange-red sand dunes stand tall in Africa's Namib Desert.

Dust devils

When desert ground gets hot, the air above it heats up. It begins swirling and forms spirals. If dust or sand is sucked into these whirlwinds, they're known as dust devils or sand devils.

Green islands

When an underground spring seeps up to the surface of the desert, an island of greenery can grow around it, called an oasis. This is the Huacachina Oasis in Peru.

Fast facts

The driest place on Earth is the Atacama Desert in Chile, where sometimes it doesn't rain for a whole year!

Too little rain and the cutting down of too many trees can dry up land until it turns into a desert. This is called desertification.

Living in a desert

Storing water can help a plant or an animal to survive in a desert. Cactus plants store precious water in their thick stems.

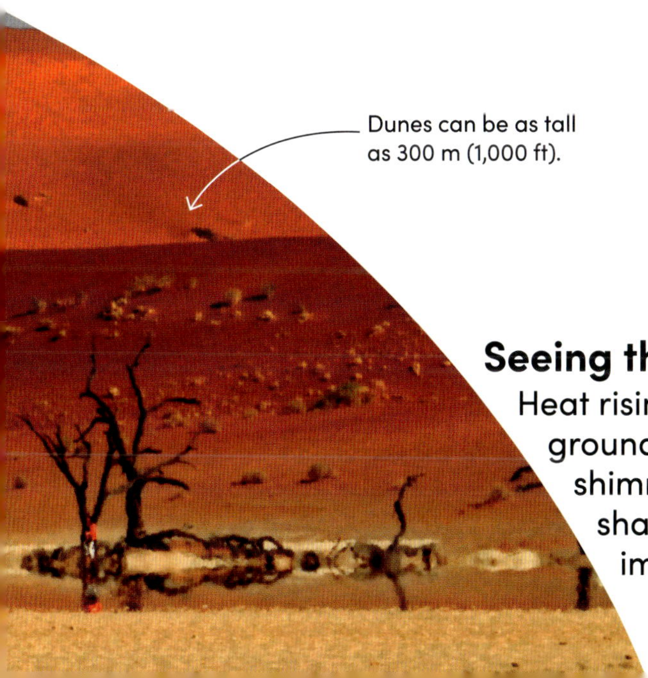

Dunes can be as tall as 300 m (1,000 ft).

Seeing things

Heat rising up from the ground can make light shimmer so it looks like shallow water. This false image is called a mirage.

What on Earth?

You're walking down the street on a warm, sunny day, and without any warning the skies grow dark and down pours mud! No matter how much we learn about the weather, it can still come up with a few surprises.

Dried out

The weather can go from low rain and warm air to no rain and extreme heat. The lack of rain brings drought.

During a drought, the soil hardens and cracks.

Fast facts

A drought occurs when there is little rainfall, which creates a water shortage.

A wildfire is an uncontrollable fire that burns through a forest or grassland. It can be sparked by lightning, but most wildfires are started accidentally by humans.

Blazing heat

Forests and grasslands may catch fire in very hot and dry weather. Dry wood and leaves burn quickly, giving rise to a runaway blaze that is hard to put out.

Exploding Earth

When liquid rock (magma), hot gas, ash, and dust burst through Earth's surface, we call it a volcano. A 2013 eruption of Mount Etna, Italy, released a towering column of ash and dust (left) that spread out over the region.

Around 60 volcanoes erupt each year.

Wet ash hardens like concrete when it dries.

It's raining mud!

When dust or volcanic ash mix with rain, the result is falling mud. Here, mud rain falls after an eruption of Mount Merapi in Indonesia, in 2010.

Predicting weather

Nobody likes having a picnic in the rain, or going to the seaside when it's cold and cloudy. To help us make plans, we depend on weather forecasts. Daily forecasts are quite accurate, but working out what the weather will do over longer periods is much harder.

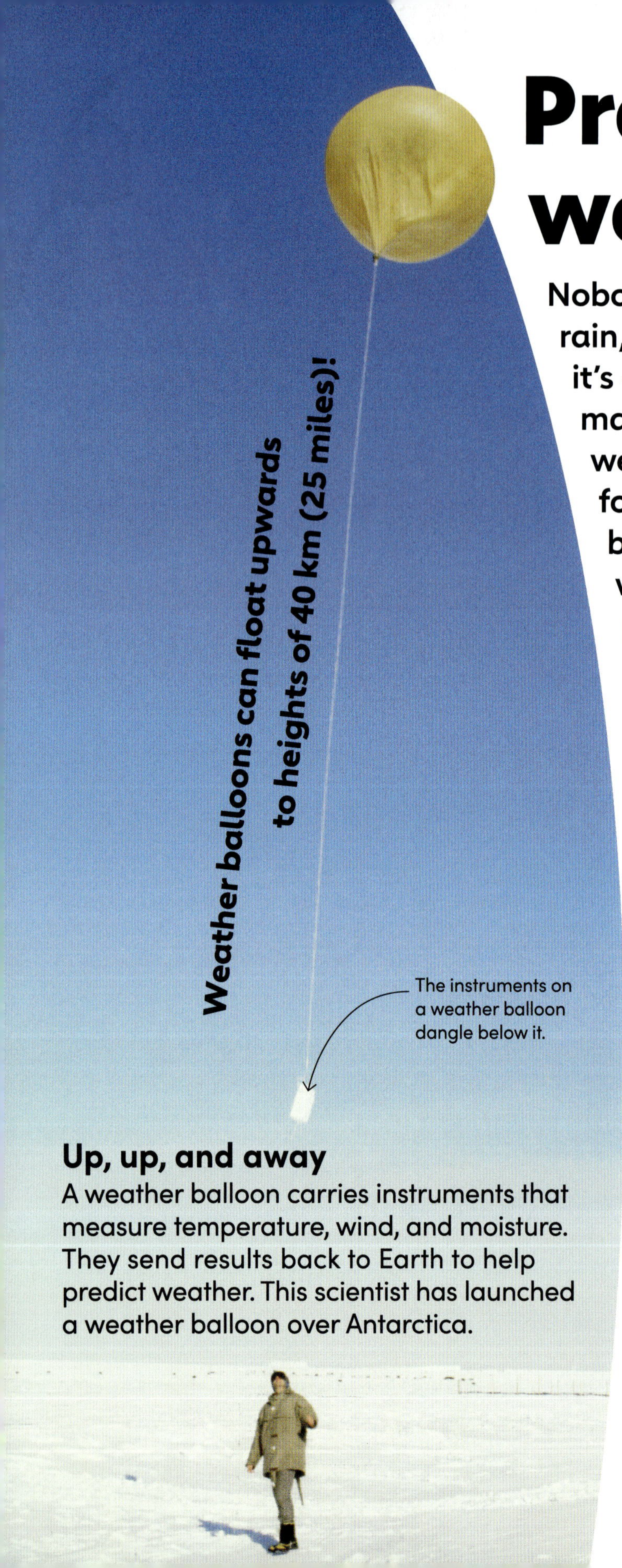

Weather balloons can float upwards to heights of 40 km (25 miles)!

Up, up, and away

A weather balloon carries instruments that measure temperature, wind, and moisture. They send results back to Earth to help predict weather. This scientist has launched a weather balloon over Antarctica.

Weather station in Croatia

Ground stations

All over the world, weather stations gather information about the air, heat, and rain. Scientists can then forecast weather at different places.

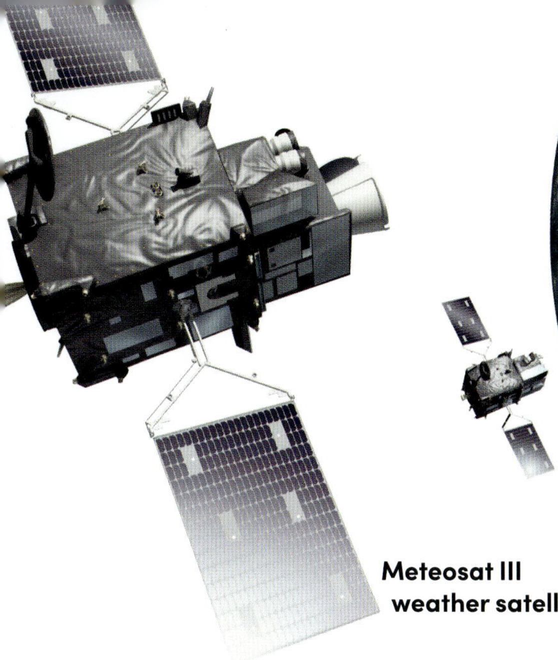

Meteosat III weather satellite

Weather watchers

Hundreds of weather satellites orbit Earth, recording pictures and data. Some move at the same speed Earth turns, so they stay above one spot. Others fly around the planet from pole to pole.

Weather from above

Images taken by Meteosat III show Earth's weather in precise detail. This picture shows clouds swirling over the Atlantic Ocean.

SUPER SENSES

Some animals can sense changes in weather better than we can. You might find wolves and dogs howling before a storm – they can detect the changes in air pressure that happen before a storm begins.

This screen shows weather patterns at a place.

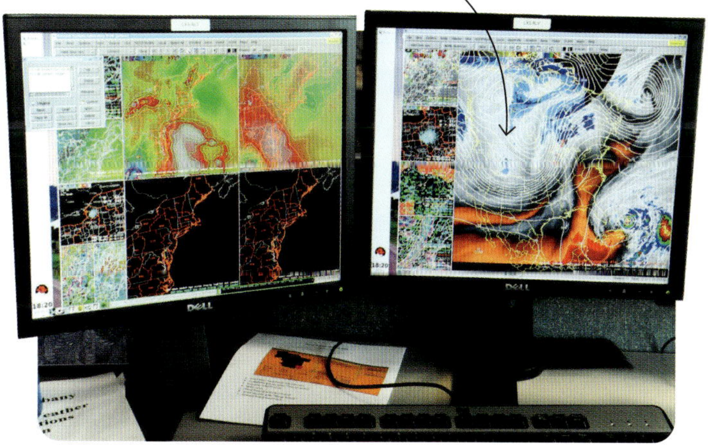

Meet the meteorologists

Scientists who study and track the weather are called meteorologists. They use computers to analyse weather data from all the available sources.

Changing climate

The Sun keeps Earth warm, helped by a blanket of air around the planet. But human actions are making it hotter than ever before. As a result, weather around the world is becoming more extreme and the ice in Earth's coldest places is melting, which causes ocean levels to rise. This is called climate change.

Greenhouse effect

A greenhouse in the garden traps heat to help plants grow. Gases such as carbon dioxide in the atmosphere work in a similar way. They trap heat, warming up our planet.

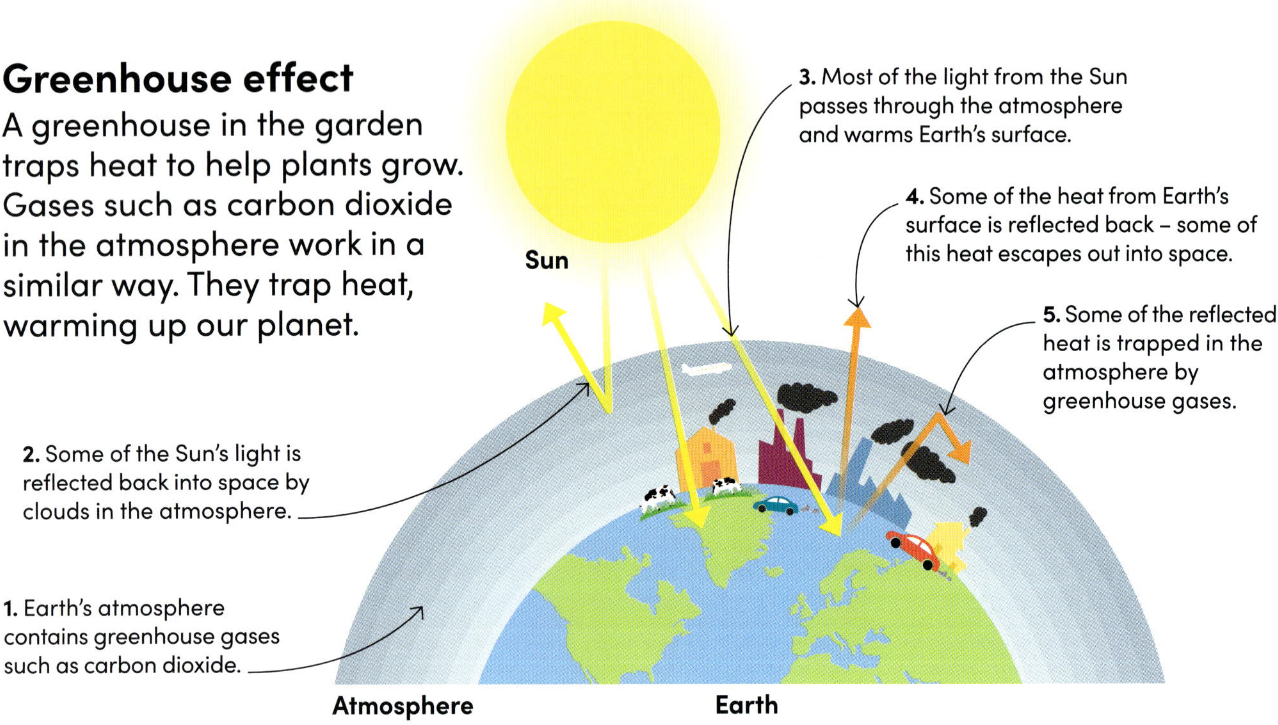

Warming our planet

Coal, oil, and gas are known as fossil fuels – they formed over millions of years, from the remains of living things. Burning them releases greenhouse gases, adding to the greenhouse effect. While part of the greenhouse effect is natural, human actions have made it more severe.

Nowhere to go

As Earth gets warmer, large chunks of polar ice are beginning to melt. This means that sea levels around the world are getting higher, and animals that live on and near the ice are losing their homes.

Every year, almost 1 trillion tonnes of ice melt on Earth because of global warming.

Fast facts

The rise in the world's temperature is called global warming.

As Earth heats up, wild weather such as stronger storms, longer droughts, and wetter winters will become more common.

Switching from fossil fuels to renewable energy sources such as solar or wind energy helps to combat climate change.

Helping our planet

Even small everyday choices can help reduce the amount of greenhouse gases we produce. Walking or cycling to school is a great way.

Harnessing weather

Imagine using sunshine to power your home! Weather is not something we can control, but we can use it to help us. Scientists use the power of weather to make cheap, clean energy.

Riding the wind

People have used the wind for thousands of years. It pushes sailing boats along lakes and seas, and can lift kites and balloons up into the air.

Farming the wind

The wind blowing over the sea helps these tall machines produce electricity. Just one of them – called a turbine – can power nearly a thousand homes. A group of turbines – on sea or land – makes up a wind farm.

Wind farm off the coast of China

Water at work

South America's Itaipu Dam is one of many big dams built across rivers to store water. The water is channelled across turbines inside the dam. As the turbines spin, they produce electricity.

Solar power is the cheapest form of energy.

The power of light

A solar power station uses mirrors to focus sunlight into a small area, heating it up. This heat turns water into steam, which helps make electricity. Morocco's Ouarzazate Solar Power Station (above) uses thousands of mirrors.

Fast facts

Electricity generated by moving water such as rivers and waterfalls is known as hydroelectric power.

Modern wind turbines can be taller than the Statue of Liberty in New York City, USA, at 150 m (490 ft)!

Which way?

You're stuck in the middle of a storm! Answer each question correctly to join your friends in the sunshine. If you get a question wrong, you can go back and try again.

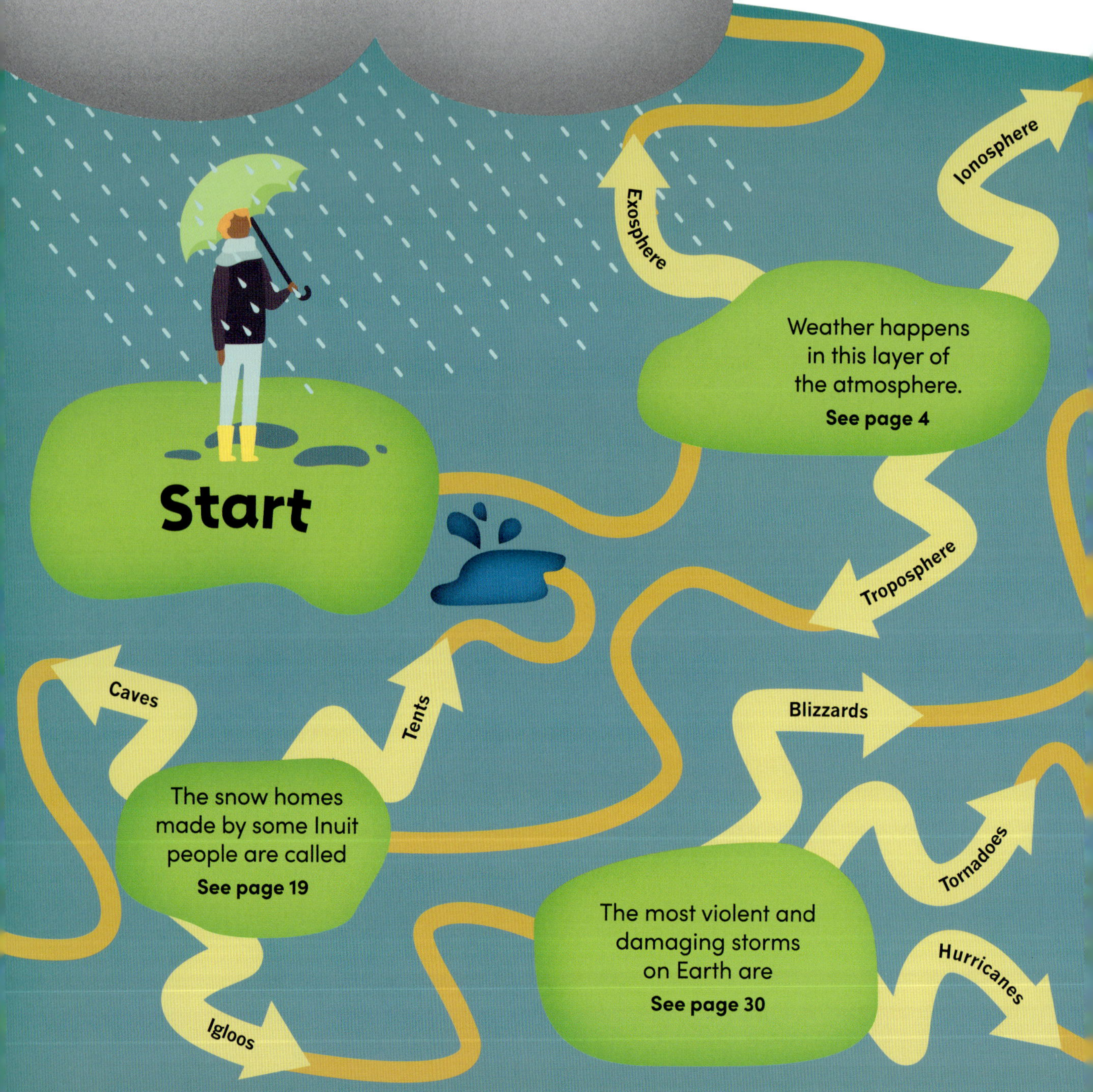

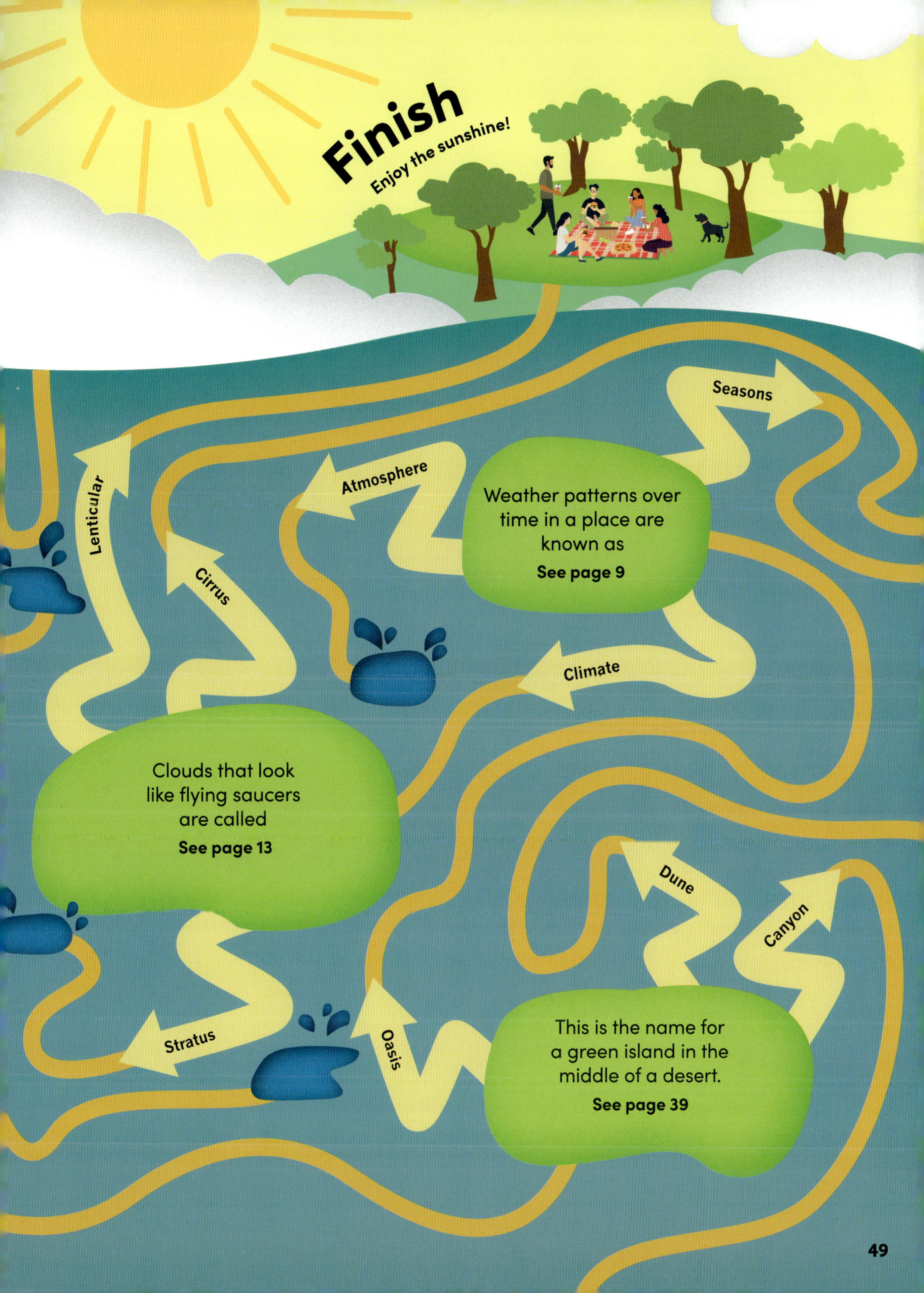
Finish
Enjoy the sunshine!
Seasons
Atmosphere
Weather patterns over time in a place are known as
See page 9
Lenticular
Cirrus
Climate
Clouds that look like flying saucers are called
See page 13
Dune
Canyon
Stratus
Oasis
This is the name for a green island in the middle of a desert.
See page 39

What's this?

Test your weather knowledge by identifying these close-up pictures. The clues should help!

1

- These clouds are shaped like lenses.
- Some people believe they look like UFOs!

2

- This is a giant shadow with a colourful halo.
- You may spot it high up on a misty mountain.

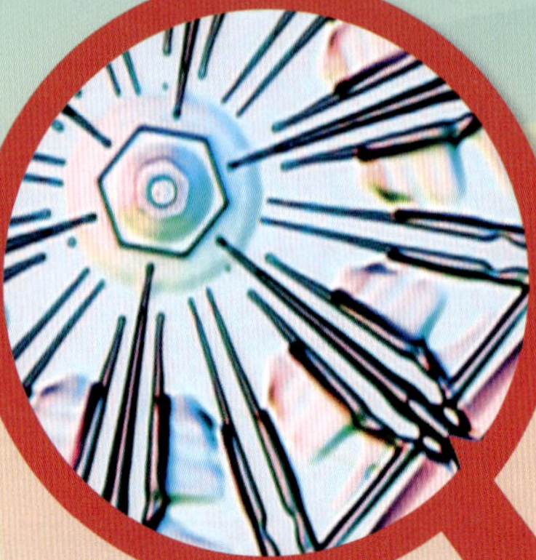

3

- A cluster of ice crystals that falls down to Earth.
- It begins as a hexagon, which grows six arms.

4

- It is a rare area of water in the desert.
- Plants grow up around the water.

5

- It is a place that makes renewable energy.
- It uses mirrors and the Sun's heat.

6

- A type of rain that is seen in some deserts.
- The rainwater does not reach the ground.

7

- This vehicle is used to track tornadoes.
- It gives scientists a quick escape route from the storm.

8

- Wispy ice that forms on rotting wood.
- It is shaped like cotton candy.

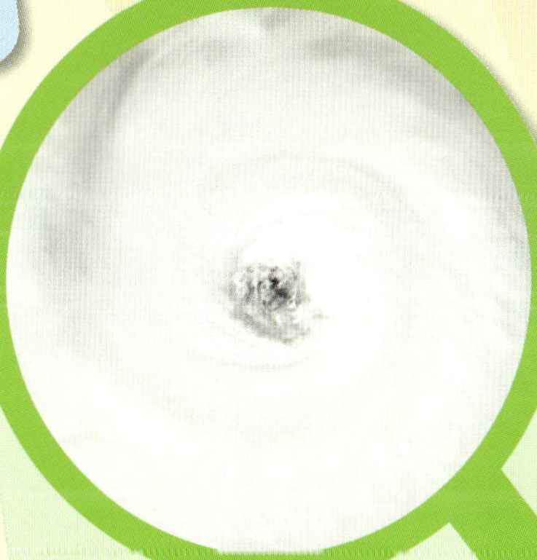

9

- It's calm here, in the centre of a hurricane.
- The fastest winds blow around it.

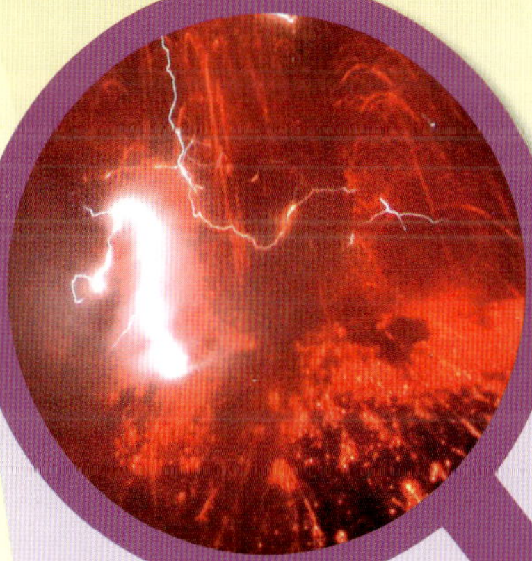

10

- A rare effect that can happen during a volcanic eruption.
- The effect happens inside the volcano's ash cloud.

Answers: 1.Lenticular clouds 2.Brocken spectre 3.Snowflake 4.Oasis 5.Solar power station 6.Virga rain 7.Radar truck 8.Hair ice 9.Eye of the storm 10.Volcanic lightning

Storm chasers

You are part of a group of scientists, driving a truck in pursuit of a tornado. Can you avoid the dangers in your path and reach the tornado safely to collect the data you need?

How to play

This is a game for up to four players.

You will need a dice and counters for each player. You could use counters from other board games you might have, or you could make your own counters with coloured paper – one colour for each player.

Each player takes turns to throw the dice, and begins from the START box. Follow the squares with each roll of the dice. If you land on an instruction, make sure you do as it says. Good luck!

Move down! **Move up!**

Real storm chasing can be dangerous and is only done by people with proper equipment and training. Always stay inside during a storm!

Glossary

Acid rain Type of rain that contains a chemical called an acid. It causes damage to the environment and buildings.

Air pressure The weight of the air in the atmosphere, pressing down on Earth.

Atmosphere Layers of air that sit between Earth's surface and outer space.

Aurora Bands of coloured light that appear in the sky over the North and South polar regions.

Blizzard Storm in which strong winds blow around snow that is falling fast and hard.

Climate change Long-term changes in Earth's temperature and weather.

Cloud Mass of water droplets or ice crystals in the sky.

Condensation Process that makes water vapour turn into liquid water.

Dew Drops of moisture that condense on the ground after a cool night.

Evaporation Process that turns water into invisible vapour in the air.

Firenado Whirlwind of hot air and fire, which can occur when a tornado passes over a wildfire.

Flash flood Flood that happens suddenly due to heavy rainfall.

Flood Water that has flowed out from a river or sea, onto what is usually dry land.

Fog Cloud that is sitting near the ground. Thin fog is called mist.

Fossil fuel Fuel, such as coal, made from animals or plants that died millions of years ago.

Freezing Process that makes water turn into solid ice at 0°C (32°F).

Frost Ice crystals that form when moisture in the air freezes.

Global warming Gradual increase in temperature around the world.

Greenhouse gas Gas that traps heat in the atmosphere. Carbon dioxide is an example.

Hail Pellets of ice that fall to the ground from storm clouds.